UP —WENT— EDMOND

BY DIANA NOONAN

ILLUSTRATED BY JENNIFER COOPER

Learning Media®

"I want a ride," said Edmond.

Monkey sat on the see-saw.
"No good," said Edmond.

Giraffe sat on the see-saw.
“No good,” said Edmond.

Lion sat on the see-saw.

"No good," said Edmond.

Zebra sat on the see-saw.
"No good," said Edmond.

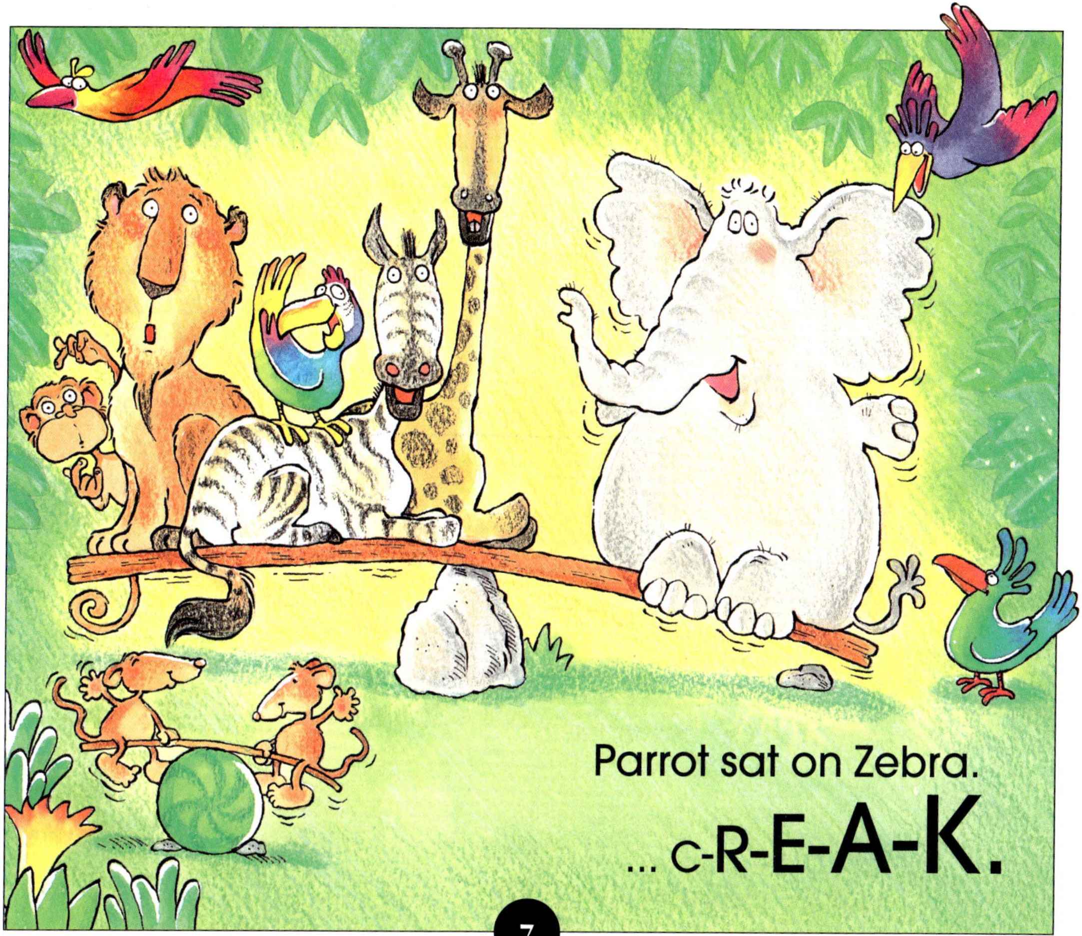

Parrot sat on Zebra.

... c-R-E-A-K.

Up went Edmond!